RANJOT SINGH CHAHAL

How to Stop Worrying and Overthinking

10 Habits to End Overthinking

Rana Books

Contents

Introduction: Understanding Overthinking

1. Defining Overthinking:

Overthinking is a cognitive process characterized by excessively analyzing rumination and deliberating on a situation problem or event. It involves dwelling on negative thoughts obsessing over minor details and constantly replaying scenarios in one's mind. Overthinkers often find it challenging to make decisions and become trapped in a cycle of worry and self-doubt.

2. How Overthinking Affects Your Life:

Overthinking can have a significant impact on various aspects of your life:

a) Paralysis by Analysis: Overthinkers tend to get stuck in a loop of overanalyzing and considering every possible outcome. This can lead to decision paralysis where they struggle to make choices fear making mistakes or constantly second-guess themselves. This can hinder personal growth career advancement and cause missed opportunities.

b) Increased Stress and Anxiety: Overthinking often involves dwelling on negative thoughts and potential worst-case scenarios. This continuous mental rumination can increase stress levels and lead to heightened anxiety. The constant worry and anticipation of negative outcomes can take a toll on mental and emotional well-being.

c) Impact on Relationships: Overthinking can negatively affect relationships. Overthinkers may overly analyze their interactions with others dissecting conversations and searching for hidden meaning in every word or action. This can lead to misinterpretations unnecessary conflict and strained relationships.

d) Impaired Problem-Solving: While it may seem counterintuitive overthinking can actually hinder problem-solving abilities. The excessive focus on minute details and potential risks can cloud judgment and prevent the individual from finding creative solutions or thinking outside the box.

e) Perfectionism and Self-Doubt: Overthinkers often have high expectations for themselves and fear making mistakes. This can result in a perfectionist mindset where nothing is ever good enough. Overthinking leads to an incessant cycle of self-doubt lowered self-confidence and a constant feeling of inadequacy.

Examples:

1. Sarah has a job interview coming up and instead of preparing effectively she spends hours overthinking every possible question the interviewers might ask analyzing her resume in detail and imagining worst-case scenarios. As a result she feels overwhelmed and anxious causing her performance to suffer during the actual interview.

2. John is constantly replaying conversations in his head trying to decipher hidden meanings and intentions behind people's words. This leads to misunderstandings and unnecessary conflicts in his relationships as he often misinterprets others' intentions and feels personally attacked.

3. Emily is a student who spends hours overanalyzing every assignment before submitting it. She constantly doubts her work edits excessively and seeks validation from others. This overthinking and perfectionism not only adds unnecessary stress but also affects her ability to meet deadlines and enjoy the learning process.

4. Mark is faced with a decision about changing careers. Instead of objectively weighing the pros and cons and trusting his intuition he obsessively researches every possible outcome further delaying his decision-making process and causing him unnecessary anxiety.

In conclusion overthinking can have detrimental effects on various aspects of one's life including decision-making emotional well-being relationships problem-solving and self-confidence. It is essential to recognize and address overthinking patterns to reduce stress improve mental health and lead a more fulfilling life.

Chapter 1: Becoming Aware of Your Overthinking Patterns

Overthinking is a common affliction that affects many people. It is the process of repeatedly and excessively thinking about a problem or situation which often leads to negative outcomes and increased stress levels. To overcome overthinking it is crucial to become aware of the underlying patterns and triggers that contribute to this thought process. In this chapter we will explore how to recognize overthinking triggers and identify negative thought patterns.

1.1 Recognizing Overthinking Triggers

One of the first steps in becoming aware of your overthinking patterns is to recognize the triggers that set off the cycle of excessive thinking. These triggers can vary from person to person but there are some common categories that many people can relate to. Here are a few examples:

1.1.1 Perfectionism: Perfectionism is a common trigger for overthinking. If you have a tendency to seek perfection in all aspects of your life you may find yourself overthinking every decision or action fearing that it won't be flawless.

For instance imagine you are working on a project at work. Instead of focusing on completing the tasks at hand you constantly worry about whether your work is good enough or if there is any room for improvement. This leads to a continuous loop of thoughts and self-doubt hindering your productivity and causing unnecessary stress.

1.1.2 Fear of Failure: Fear of failure is another significant trigger for overthinking. If you have a deep-seated fear of making mistakes or not meeting expectations you may find yourself continuously running scenarios in your mind trying to avoid any potential pitfalls.

For example let's say you are planning to start a new business venture. Instead of taking action you spend excessive amounts of time worrying about all the possible things that could go wrong. This fear of failure immobilizes you and prevents you from moving forward.

1.1.3 Negative Experiences: Negative experiences from the past can also be triggers for overthinking. If you have encountered setbacks or failures in the past you may find yourself replaying those events over and over in your mind analyzing every detail and searching for answers.

For instance imagine you had a relationship that ended badly. You may find yourself constantly ruminating on what went wrong blaming yourself or the other person and analyzing every conversation and action taken during that relationship. This constant dwelling on the past can prevent you from moving on and finding new happiness.

1.1.4 Uncertainty: Uncertainty about the future is a trigger that can lead to overthinking. When faced with unknown outcomes or ambiguous situations some individuals tend to analyze every possible scenario trying to gain a sense of control and certainty.

For example let's say you are considering a job offer in a new city. Instead of focusing on the potential positives of the opportunity you spend an excessive amount of time speculating about all the potential challenges and what-ifs. This analysis paralysis can lead to indecision and heightened anxiety.

1.2 Identifying Negative Thought Patterns

Once you have recognized the triggers that lead to overthinking the next step is to identify the negative thought patterns that perpetuate this thought process. Negative thought patterns are cognitive distortions or unhelpful thinking styles that fuel overthinking. Here are a few examples:

1.2.1 Catastrophizing: Catastrophizing is a common negative thought pattern where an individual magnifies and exaggerates the potential negative outcomes of a situation. They often jump to the worst-case scenario without considering more realistic possibilities.

For example let's say you have a minor disagreement with a friend. Instead of viewing it as a normal part of any relationship you may catastrophize the situation by thinking that your friendship is now irreparable and that you have lost a valuable connection in your life.

1.2.2 Overgeneralizing: Overgeneralizing is a cognitive distortion where a person takes one negative experience or instance and applies it to all similar situations. They make broad generalizations based on limited evidence.

For instance if you receive criticism on a presentation at work you may overgeneralize this feedback and believe that you are a terrible presenter in all contexts. This thought pattern can lead to a lack of confidence and avoidance of future opportunities.

1.2.3 Filtering: Filtering is a negative thought pattern where an individual focuses only on the negative aspects of a situation while ignoring or downplaying any positive aspects. They selectively filter out the positive information and amplify the negative.

For example imagine you receive a performance evaluation at work and receive five positive comments and one constructive criticism. Instead of acknowledging the positive feedback you hyper-focus on the one negative comment disregarding the overall positive evaluation.

1.2.4 Personalization: Personalization is a cognitive distortion where an individual takes things personally and assumes responsibility for events or situations that are beyond their control. They attribute blame to themselves even when other factors may be involved.

For instance if a friend cancels plans at the last minute you may internalize their actions and assume that they no longer want to spend time with you because of something you did. This thought pattern can lead to feelings of guilt and insecurity.

1.2.5 All-or-Nothing Thinking: All-or-nothing thinking is a cognitive distortion where a person perceives situations in extremes with no middle ground. They view everything as either black or white ignoring the shades of gray.

For example if you receive feedback on a project at work that includes both positive and negative aspects you may only focus on the negative aspects and discount the positive elements. This rigid thinking pattern can lead to a skewed perception of reality.

In conclusion becoming aware of your overthinking patterns requires recognizing the triggers that set off excessive thinking and identifying the negative thought patterns that perpetuate this cycle. By understanding these patterns you can begin to take steps towards reducing overthinking and living a more balanced and peaceful life.

Chapter 2: Cultivating Mindfulness

- The Power of Mindfulness in Overcoming Overthinking

Overthinking is a common mental habit that many people struggle with. It involves dwelling on past events or worrying about future outcomes often leading to heightened stress and anxiety. However cultivating mindfulness can be a powerful tool in overcoming overthinking and finding inner peace.

Mindfulness is the practice of being fully present and aware of one's thoughts feelings and sensations in the present moment without judgment. By developing mindfulness individuals can learn to observe their thoughts without becoming entangled in them allowing them to break free from the cycle of overthinking.

One of the key aspects of mindfulness is learning to detach oneself from thoughts. Often overthinking occurs when individuals become excessively identified with their thoughts believing them to be true and allowing them to dictate their emotions and actions. Through mindfulness one can develop the ability to observe thoughts as passing events rather than absolute truths. This detachment enables individuals to gain a different perspective on their thoughts and prevents them from being overwhelmed by them.

For example suppose you have an important work presentation coming up and you find yourself constantly worrying about forgetting something or not performing well. Without mindfulness you might get caught up in these thoughts leading to increased anxiety and decreased focus. However by practicing mindfulness you can observe those worrying thoughts as temporary events and choose not to engage with them fully. This allows you to redirect your attention back to the present moment and focus on the task at hand reducing overthinking and promoting a more positive mindset.

Another way mindfulness helps overcome overthinking is by cultivating a non-judgmental attitude towards thoughts and emotions. Often overthinkers become critical of their own thoughts judging them as excessive irrational or unhelpful. This self-judgment can further perpetuate the overthinking cycle as individuals feel guilty or ashamed for having such thoughts. However mindfulness encourages individuals to accept their thoughts and emotions as they are without judgment.

For instance let's say you made a mistake at work and you start overthinking about the possible consequences and what others might think of you. Instead of judging yourself for having these thoughts mindfulness allows you to acknowledge them with compassion and understanding. By accepting your thoughts without judgment you can detach from them more easily and choose not to get entangled in overthinking.

Moreover mindfulness helps individuals develop an increased

awareness of their thoughts and patterns of overthinking. By practicing mindfulness regularly individuals can become more attuned to the triggers and patterns that lead to overthinking. This heightened self-awareness allows them to intervene and redirect their thoughts before they spiral into overthinking.

For example let's say you often find yourself overthinking during your commute to work. By practicing mindfulness you become aware of the triggers such as passing certain landmarks or specific thoughts that arise during that time. With this awareness you can proactively redirect your attention to the present moment engaging in mindfulness techniques such as focusing on your breath or observing your surroundings. By doing so you can prevent the overthinking cycle from taking hold and cultivate a calmer state of mind.

- Practical Strategies to Develop Mindfulness
    Developing mindfulness is a gradual process that requires consistent practice and dedication. Here are some practical strategies to cultivate mindfulness in your daily life:

1. Mindful Breathing: Deep breathing exercises are an effective way to anchor oneself in the present moment. Take a few moments throughout the day to focus on your breath observing each inhale and exhale. This simple practice helps calm the mind and brings attention back to the present.

2. Body Scan Meditation: Body scan meditation involves system-atically bringing awareness to each part of the body from head to toe. As you scan through each body part notice any sensations and observe them without judgment. This practice enhances

bodily awareness and cultivates mindfulness.

3. Mindful Eating: Instead of rushing through meals practice mindful eating by paying attention to the taste texture and aroma of each bite. Engage all your senses and savor the experience fully. This practice encourages present-moment awareness and helps develop a healthy relationship with food.

4. Mindful Walking: Take a walk outdoors and pay attention to each step the sensation of your feet touching the ground and the surrounding environment. Notice the sights sounds and smells around you. This practice fosters a sense of grounding and connection with the present moment.

5. Mindful Journaling: Set aside a few minutes each day to write down your thoughts and feelings without judgment. Use this time to reflect on your experiences observe any patterns of overthinking and express gratitude for the present moment. Journaling promotes self-awareness and reflection.

6. Mindful Pause: Throughout the day take intentional pauses to check in with yourself. During these moments observe your thoughts emotions and physical sensations without reacting to them. This practice helps create a mental space between stimuli and response allowing for more conscious decision-making.

7. Mindfulness Apps and Resources: Utilize smartphone apps and online resources that offer guided mindfulness meditations such as Headspace Calm or Insight Timer. These tools provide structured guidance and support for developing mindfulness.

8. Mindful Listening: Practice active listening in conversations by giving your full attention to the other person. Avoid interrupting or formulating responses in your mind while they are speaking. Truly listen to their words tone and body language fostering deeper connections and presence in interpersonal interactions.

9. Mindfulness in Daily Activities: Infuse mindfulness into daily activities such as brushing your teeth washing dishes or taking a shower. Instead of engaging in autopilot mode bring your attention to the sensations movements and details of each activity. This practice brings mindfulness into everyday life.

10. Mindfulness Retreats and Classes: Consider attending mindfulness retreats or enrolling in mindfulness-based stress reduction (MBSR) classes. These formal programs offer immersive experiences and guidance from experienced teachers providing a supportive environment for deepening mindfulness practice.

Remember developing mindfulness takes time and patience. Start by incorporating small doses of mindfulness into your daily routine and gradually increase the duration and frequency of your practices. With consistent effort mindfulness will become an integral part of your life helping you overcome overthinking and cultivate a sense of inner peace and well-being.

Chapter 3: Practicing Self-Compassion

Reducing Self-Criticism and Judgment – Building a Kind Empathetic Inner Dialogue

Introduction:

In our journey of personal growth and self-improvement it is crucial to cultivate self-compassion. Self-compassion entails treating ourselves with the same kindness and understanding that we would offer to a loved one who is struggling. Many of us tend to engage in self-criticism and judgment which can hinder our progress and negatively impact our mental well-being. However by learning to reduce self-criticism and judgment and building a kind and empathetic inner dialogue we can foster self-compassion and create a more positive relationship with ourselves. This chapter will delve into the importance of self-compassion and provide practical strategies and examples for reducing self-criticism judgment and cultivating a kind and empathetic inner dialogue.

1. Understanding Self-Criticism and Judgment:

Self-criticism refers to the tendency to evaluate and criticize ourselves harshly often driven by the fear of failure or the desire for perfection. It involves negative self-talk focusing excessively on our weaknesses and comparing ourselves unfavorably to others. Judgment on the other hand involves forming negative opinions about ourselves based on our perceived inadequacies or failures. Both self-criticism and judgment can undermine our self-esteem hinder personal growth and perpetuate a cycle of negativity.

Example 1:

Sarah a recent college graduate has been struggling to find a job in her desired field. Instead of viewing this setback as a normal part of the job search process she is consumed by self-criticism. She constantly tells herself "You're not good enough "You should have done better and "You'll never succeed." This self-critical mindset leaves Sarah feeling discouraged lowers her motivation and prevents her from exploring alternative opportunities.

2. The Impact of Self-Criticism and Judgment:

Engaging in self-criticism and judgment can have detrimental effects on our emotional well-being and mental health. It can lead to increased stress anxiety and depression. When we constantly berate ourselves we set unrealistic expectations and are more likely to experience feelings of worthlessness and inadequacy. Additionally self-criticism and judgment can hinder our personal growth as they focus more on our flaws and failures rather than our strengths and achievements.

Example 2:

John a talented musician has been invited to perform at a local event. However due to his fear of making mistakes and being judged by others he finds himself paralyzed by self-criticism.

He replays negative thoughts such as "You'll mess up "Nobody will like your performance and "You're not good enough." As a result John's anxiety intensifies and he ultimately decides to decline the opportunity missing out on a chance to showcase his talent and gain valuable experience.

3. Cultivating Self-Compassion:

Self-compassion involves treating ourselves with kindness understanding and acceptance particularly in the face of difficulties or failures. It means recognizing our shared humanity acknowledging that everyone makes mistakes and embracing ourselves with warmth and compassion. By cultivating self-compassion we can reduce self-criticism and judgment foster resilience and promote overall well-being.

Example 3:

Emma a new mother is experiencing feelings of guilt and self-doubt. Despite her best efforts she often compares herself to other mothers who seem to have it all together. To combat her self-critical thoughts Emma starts practicing self-compassion. Instead of berating herself when she struggles she reminds herself that it is normal to face challenges as a new parent and acknowledges that she is doing her best. This self-compassionate mindset helps Emma alleviate her guilt and allows her to focus on nurturing her child instead of obsessing over perfection.

4. Strategies for Reducing Self-Criticism and Judgment:
4.1 Practice Mindfulness:
Mindfulness involves being present in the moment and observing our thoughts and emotions without judgment. By cultivating mindfulness we can become aware of our self-critical

thoughts and redirect our attention to the present moment. This helps us avoid getting caught in a spiral of negativity and self-judgment.

Example 4:

Chris a recent divorcee often experiences thoughts like "I'm a failure "No one will ever love me and "It's all my fault." To reduce self-criticism Chris begins practicing mindfulness meditation. During meditation he observes his thoughts without attaching any judgment to them. Gradually he realizes that these self-critical thoughts are merely patterns of the mind and do not define his worth as a person. By practicing mindfulness regularly Chris can better manage his self-critical thoughts and build a more compassionate inner dialogue.

4.2 Challenge Negative Thought Patterns:

Another effective strategy for reducing self-criticism and judgment is to challenge our negative thought patterns. We often accept self-critical thoughts as facts but by questioning their validity we can gain a more balanced perspective and cultivate self-compassion.

Example 5:

Maria a college student often struggles with self-esteem issues and frequently judges her appearance. When she catches herself thinking "I look ugly she pauses and asks herself "Is this thought grounded in reality?" Often Maria realizes that her negative self-perception is influenced by societal standards of beauty. By challenging these thoughts and reminding herself of her unique qualities and strengths she can reduce self-judgment and build a more compassionate inner dialogue.

4.3 Practice Self-Validation:

Self-validation involves acknowledging our feelings experiences and efforts in a compassionate and supportive manner. By validating ourselves we counteract self-criticism and judgment and foster self-acceptance and self-worth.

Example 6:

Mike a professional athlete has recently been struggling with a series of losses. Instead of engaging in self-criticism he practices self-validation by acknowledging his efforts and reminding himself that setbacks are a natural part of the journey toward success. Mike says to himself "It's okay to feel disappointed but remember the hard work and dedication you put into training. You're doing your best and that's what matters." This self-validation helps Mike maintain a positive mindset and motivates him to keep pushing forward.

5. Building a Kind Empathetic Inner Dialogue:

5.1 Practice Self-Compassionate Language:

Developing a kind and empathetic inner dialogue requires using self-compassionate language when talking to ourselves. Instead of berating ourselves we can speak to ourselves with kindness and understanding as we would to a close friend who is struggling. This cultivates self-compassion and fosters a more positive relationship with ourselves.

Example 7:

Michelle a business professional has made a mistake at work that cost the company money. Instead of engaging in self-criticism she chooses to use self-compassionate language. She says to herself "It's understandable that you made a mistake.

Everyone makes them sometimes. What matters is how you learn from this experience and improve in the future." By using self-compassionate language Michelle reframes her mistake as an opportunity for growth and development.

5.2 Cultivate Self-Affirming Affirmations:

Self-affirmations are positive statements we repeat to ourselves to counteract negative self-talk and cultivate self-compassion. By regularly practicing self-affirmations we can challenge self-criticism build self-esteem and foster a more compassionate inner dialogue.

Example 8:

Liam a student preparing for important exams often doubts his abilities and fears failure. To counteract these self-critical thoughts Liam creates self-affirmations such as "I am capable and prepared "I have the knowledge and skills to succeed and "I believe in my ability to overcome challenges." By repeating these affirmations daily Liam strengthens his self-belief and reduces self-judgment allowing him to approach exams with greater confidence.

Conclusion:

Practicing self-compassion is essential for personal growth emotional well-being and cultivating a positive relationship with ourselves. By reducing self-criticism and judgment and building a kind and empathetic inner dialogue we can nurture self-compassion foster resilience and promote overall mental health. Through strategies such as mindfulness challenging negative thought patterns practicing self-validation using self-compassionate language and cultivating self-affirmations we can embrace ourselves with greater kindness understanding and acceptance. By practicing these techniques consistently we can develop a compassionate relationship with ourselves and create a foundation for personal well-being and success.

Chapter 4: Reframing Negative Thoughts

In this chapter we will explore techniques for challenging and restructuring negative thoughts. Our thoughts have a profound impact on our emotions behaviors and overall well-being. Often negative thoughts can be distorted and irrational leading to unnecessary stress anxiety and unhappiness. By learning to identify and reframe these negative thoughts we can cultivate a more positive and empowering mindset. Additionally we will discuss the application of positive affirmations to reinforce and nurture positive thinking patterns.

Section 1: Cognitive Distortions

Cognitive distortions are patterns of irrational and negative thinking that can distort our perception of reality. These distortions often arise automatically and unconsciously leading to negative emotions and self-defeating behaviors. By becoming aware of these distortions and challenging them we can replace them with more balanced and realistic thoughts.

1. All-or-Nothing Thinking:
This cognitive distortion involves viewing situations in black

and white terms without recognizing shades of gray or middle ground. For example someone may perceive themselves as a complete failure simply because they did not achieve one particular goal. To reframe this it is important to recognize and acknowledge the progress made and the areas of success rather than falling into the trap of focusing solely on the negatives.

2. Overgeneralization:

Overgeneralization occurs when we draw broad conclusions based on isolated incidents or single instances of negative experiences. For instance someone who is rejected by one potential romantic partner may conclude that they will never find love. It is important to challenge this distortion by reminding ourselves that one negative experience does not dictate our future.

3. Mental Filtering:

Mental filtering involves selectively focusing only on the negative aspects of a situation while ignoring or downplaying any positive aspects. This can lead to a skewed perception of reality where one is constantly fixated on the negatives. To challenge this distortion it is crucial to consciously shift our focus towards the positive aspects and practice gratitude for the things that are going well in our lives.

4. Discounting the Positive:

Discounting the positive is a distortion where we downplay or dismiss positive experiences or attributes as if they don't count. For example if someone receives praise for their work they may dismiss it as just being lucky or not deserving of recognition. To reframe this distortion it is necessary to acknowledge and appreciate our positive qualities and accomplishments.

5. Catastrophizing:

Catastrophizing involves blowing situations out of proportion and expecting the worst-case scenario to happen. This distortion can lead to excessive worry and anxiety. To challenge this distortion it is beneficial to assess the situation objectively and consider alternative more realistic outcomes.

6. Personalization:

Personalization occurs when we assume excessive responsibility for negative events blaming ourselves for things that are beyond our control. For example someone may blame themselves entirely for a failed relationship disregarding external factors that contributed to the outcome. To challenge this distortion it is important to recognize and accept that not everything is within our control and that other factors may have influenced the situation.

7. Emotional Reasoning:

Emotional reasoning involves assuming that our feelings accurately reflect reality. For example someone may feel anxious about an upcoming presentation and conclude that it will inevitably go poorly. To challenge this distortion it is essential to recognize that our feelings are not always an accurate reflection of the truth and that we can actively work to change our thoughts and beliefs.

Section 2: Challenging and Restructuring Cognitive Distortions

Challenging and restructuring cognitive distortions requires a deliberate and systematic approach. Here are some strategies that can be employed to challenge and reframe negative thoughts:

1. Recognize Negative Thoughts:
The first step is to become aware of the negative thoughts that arise in our minds. This can be done by paying attention to our internal dialogue and identifying patterns of negative thinking. Journaling our thoughts can be particularly helpful in this process.

2. Gather Evidence:
Once negative thoughts have been identified it is important to gather evidence that supports or contradicts them. This can involve asking ourselves questions such as "What evidence do I have to support this thought "Is there any evidence that contradicts this thought and "Are there any alternative explanations or perspectives?"

3. Generate Alternative Thoughts:
Based on the gathered evidence we can begin to generate alternative thoughts that are more balanced and realistic. These thoughts should challenge the distortions and offer a more accurate and constructive perspective. For example if the negative thought is "I never succeed at anything an alternative thought could be "I have succeeded in the past and can learn from my failures."

4. Reality Testing:
To further strengthen the alternative thoughts it is important to test their validity against reality. This can involve seeking objective feedback from trusted friends or professionals examining past experiences for evidence or conducting research to gather

relevant information. The goal is to ensure that the alternative thoughts are rooted in reality and are not simply a way to avoid the truth.

5. Practice and Reinforce:

Restructuring negative thoughts requires continuous practice and repetition. The more we actively challenge and replace negative thoughts with more positive and realistic ones the more ingrained these new thought patterns will become. It is important to be patient and consistent in this process as change takes time.

Section 3: Utilizing Positive Affirmations

Positive affirmations are positive statements that we can repeat to ourselves to build self-confidence self-esteem and a positive mindset. They serve as powerful tools to counteract negative self-talk and reinforce positive thinking patterns. Here are some guidelines for utilizing positive affirmations effectively:

1. Identify and Address Negative Self-Talk:

To effectively use positive affirmations it is important to first identify and address any negative self-talk or negative beliefs that we hold about ourselves. This can involve exploring our underlying beliefs and challenging them with evidence and alternative perspectives.

2. Create Personalized Positive Affirmations:

Positive affirmations should be tailored to our specific needs and goals. They should reflect the positive qualities and attributes we want to reinforce within ourselves. For example if someone struggles with self-confidence a positive affirmation could be "I am confident and capable in all that I do."

3. Use Present Tense and Positive Language:
Positive affirmations should be stated in the present tense and expressed in positive language. This helps to reprogram our subconscious mind and reinforce positive beliefs about ourselves. Instead of saying "I will be confident it is more effective to say "I am confident."

4. Repeat Regularly and Consistently:
To derive maximum benefit from positive affirmations they need to be repeated regularly and consistently. This can involve setting aside dedicated time each day to repeat affirmations writing them down or creating visual reminders. Consistency is key in strengthening and internalizing positive beliefs.

5. Visualize and Embrace the Affirmations:
While repeating positive affirmations it is helpful to visualize ourselves embodying the qualities and attributes described in the affirmations. By engaging our imagination and emotions we can create a stronger connection between the affirmations and our subconscious mind. Embracing the affirmations with conviction and belief is crucial for their effectiveness.

Conclusion:

Challenging and restructuring negative thoughts as well as utilizing positive affirmations are powerful techniques for cultivating a more positive and empowering mindset. By becoming aware of cognitive distortions and replacing them with more balanced and realistic thoughts we can reduce stress anxiety and unhappiness. Positive affirmations serve as tools to reinforce positive thinking patterns and build self-confidence. The key to these techniques is consistent practice and repetition. With time and effort we can reshape our thoughts and beliefs leading to a more fulfilling and joyful life.

Chapter 5: Implementing Effective Decision-Making Techniques

Section 1: Overcoming Analysis Paralysis

One common challenge in the decision-making process is analysis paralysis which refers to the state of being unable to make a decision due to overthinking and excessive analysis. This can result in wasting valuable time and resources and can hinder progress. To overcome analysis paralysis and make effective decisions it is important to implement certain strategies and techniques. In this section we will explore some practical approaches to combat analysis paralysis.

1. Define Clear Decision Criteria: Before embarking on the decision-making process it is crucial to define clear decision criteria. This involves identifying the key factors and requirements that should be considered when evaluating options. For example if you are deciding on purchasing a new car you may consider factors such as budget fuel efficiency safety features and car size. By setting clear decision criteria you can narrow down your options and simplify the decision-making process.

2. Gather Relevant Information: To make well-informed deci-

sions it is important to gather relevant information. This may involve conducting research seeking expert opinions and collecting data related to the decision at hand. However it is essential to strike a balance between gathering enough information and not getting overwhelmed by an excess of data. Focus on obtaining the most relevant and reliable information that will help you evaluate your options effectively.

3. Set a Time Limit: Analysis paralysis often occurs when there is no deadline for making a decision. Setting a time limit can help overcome this challenge by creating a sense of urgency. Determine a reasonable timeframe for making the decision and commit to making a choice within that timeframe. This will motivate you to prioritize your analysis and avoid getting caught in an endless cycle of overthinking.

4. Break Down the Decision: Complex decisions can be overwhelming leading to analysis paralysis. To tackle this break down the decision into smaller more manageable components. For instance if you are deciding on which software to purchase for your business break it down into factors such as cost features customer reviews and compatibility. By addressing each component separately you can focus on one aspect at a time and make progress towards a decision.

5. Use Decision-Making Tools and Techniques: Various decision-making tools and techniques are available that can help overcome analysis paralysis. Some commonly used techniques include:

a. Decision Matrix: This tool allows you to compare options

based on multiple criteria. You assign weights to each criterion and rate each option accordingly. By systematically evaluating each option the decision matrix can provide a quantifiable basis for making a decision.

b. SWOT Analysis: SWOT stands for Strengths Weaknesses Opportunities and Threats. This technique involves analyzing an option's internal strengths and weaknesses as well as external opportunities and threats. SWOT analysis can help you gain a comprehensive understanding of the factors influencing your decision.

c. Pros and Cons List: Creating a pros and cons list is a simple yet effective technique. Write down the advantages and disadvantages of each option and weigh their importance. This method can help you visualize the trade-offs associated with each choice and guide your decision-making process.

6. Trust Your Instincts: While it is essential to gather information and analyze options sometimes it is necessary to trust your instincts. Intuition can play a valuable role in decision-making especially when faced with complex or ambiguous situations. Allow yourself to tap into your gut feelings as they can provide insights that analysis alone may not reveal. However it is important not to rely solely on instinct but to consider it in conjunction with the gathered information and rational analysis.

Section 2: Strategies for Making Confident Choices

Confidence is a key factor in effective decision-making. When you lack confidence in your choices it becomes challenging to take decisive actions and commit to a particular path. In this section we will explore strategies to build confidence and make confident choices.

1. Clarify Your Values and Priorities: Aligning your decisions with your values and priorities can boost your confidence. Take some time to reflect on what is important to you and what you want to achieve. By knowing your values and priorities you can make decisions that align with your goals giving you a greater sense of confidence and purpose.

2. Seek Input and Feedback: Seeking input from others can provide valuable perspectives and insights. Engage in discussions with trusted individuals who have relevant knowledge or expertise in the area of your decision. Their input can help you consider different viewpoints and identify blind spots. Additionally receiving feedback on your ideas and proposed choices can enhance your confidence in your decision-making process.

3. Embrace Failure as a Learning Opportunity: Fear of failure can paralyze decision-making and erode confidence. Instead of viewing failure as a negative outcome see it as an opportunity for growth and learning. Understand that not every decision will yield the desired outcome but each decision is a chance to learn adapt and improve. Embracing a growth mindset can help you approach decision-making with more confidence and resilience.

4. Visualize Success: Visualization is a powerful tool to enhance confidence. Take the time to visualize the positive outcomes

of your choices. Imagine yourself successfully executing the decision and achieving the desired results. Visualizing success can reinforce your confidence and motivate you to move forward with your chosen option.

5. Take Incremental Steps: Making a big irreversible decision can be intimidating and lead to hesitation. Breaking down the decision into smaller incremental steps can help build confidence. Instead of making a one-time all-or-nothing decision consider taking smaller actions that allow you to gather feedback and assess the outcome. By gradually building momentum and confidence through small wins you can make more confident choices.

6. Reflect and Learn from Past Decisions: Look back at the decisions you have made in the past and evaluate their outcomes. Consider what went well and what could have been improved. Reflecting on past successes and failures can provide valuable lessons and insights. By learning from your past decisions you can refine your decision-making skills and approach future choices with increased confidence.

7. Practice Decision-Making: Confidence in decision-making grows with practice. Seek opportunities to make decisions both big and small and take responsibility for the consequences. As you make more decisions and gain experience you will become more comfortable and confident in your ability to make informed choices. Remember that making no decision at all is also a decision and actively engaging in decision-making will enable you to build confidence over time.

Conclusion:

Overcoming analysis paralysis and making confident choices are essential skills for effective decision-making. By implementing strategies to combat analysis paralysis such as defining clear decision criteria gathering relevant information setting a time limit breaking down the decision utilizing decision-making tools and trusting your instincts you can make decisions more efficiently. Additionally building confidence through strategies such as clarifying your values seeking input and feedback embracing failure as a learning opportunity visualizing success taking incremental steps reflecting and learning from past decisions and practicing decision-making you can make choices with conviction and assurance. Remember that decision-making is a continuous process and the more you engage in it the better you become at navigating complex situations and making effective decisions.

Chapter 6: Setting Boundaries and Prioritizing

Establishing Healthy Boundaries with Others:

Setting healthy boundaries is crucial for maintaining healthy relationships managing stress and promoting self-care. It involves clearly defining what is acceptable and unacceptable in your interactions with others as well as understanding and respecting the boundaries set by others. By establishing healthy boundaries you can protect your physical and emotional well-being maintain your personal values and achieve a balance between your own needs and the needs of others.

1. Define your boundaries: Start by identifying your values needs and limits. Reflect on what is important to you and what makes you feel comfortable. Consider areas such as personal space emotional boundaries time and energy limits and communication styles. For example you may decide that you need alone time every day to recharge or that you don't want to engage in gossip or negative conversations.

2. Communicate your boundaries: Once you have defined your boundaries it's essential to communicate them effectively to

others. Be clear assertive and respectful when expressing your limits. Use "I" statements to express how their behavior affects you rather than making accusations or blaming them. For instance instead of saying "You always invade my personal space you can say "I feel uncomfortable when someone gets too close to me."

3. Set consequences: Boundaries are meaningless without consequences. Communicate specific consequences if someone violates your boundaries. This helps ensure that your boundaries are respected and reinforces the importance of maintaining them. For example if someone continues to disrespect your boundaries you may choose to spend less time with them or distance yourself from the relationship.

4. Be consistent and firm: Consistency is key when setting boundaries. People might test your boundaries especially if they're used to you not having clearly defined limits. Stay firm and maintain your boundaries even when faced with resistance or pushback. Remember it's your right to set your own boundaries and prioritize your well-being.

5. Respect others' boundaries: Just as you expect others to respect your boundaries it's equally important to respect theirs. Listen actively pay attention to their needs and adjust your behavior accordingly. Avoid crossing their limits and be mindful of how your actions or words may impact them. By fostering a culture of mutual respect you can strengthen relationships and create a healthier and more balanced environment.

Prioritizing Tasks and Managing Time Effectively:

With the increasing demands of work personal obligations and various responsibilities effective time management and task prioritization are essential skills. By organizing tasks based on importance and allocating time wisely you can enhance productivity reduce stress and achieve a greater sense of accomplishment.

1. Identify your priorities: Start by clarifying your goals and determining what tasks and activities align with them. Prioritize tasks based on their importance and urgency. Use tools like to-do lists or task management apps to keep track of your priorities. Assigning deadlines to each task can also help you stay on track and avoid procrastination.

2. Eliminate time-wasting activities: Identify activities that consume a significant amount of your time but add little value to your life or goals. These may include excessive social media use constant checking of emails or spending excessive time on non-essential tasks. Minimize or eliminate these time-wasters to create more space for important activities.

3. Delegate and seek help: Recognize that you don't have to do everything yourself. Delegate tasks that can be handled by others whether it's at work or in your personal life. Delegation not only lightens your load but also provides opportunities for others to develop their skills and contribute to the team. Additionally don't hesitate to seek help when needed. Asking for assistance can save time and prevent burnout.

4. Break tasks into manageable chunks: Large tasks can be overwhelming and may lead to procrastination. Break them

down into smaller more manageable tasks. Set achievable milestones and work on them one by one. This approach allows you to focus on specific parts of a task makes progress more tangible and boosts motivation.

5. Prioritize self-care: Taking care of yourself is a priority. Self-care activities such as exercise mindfulness and relaxation are essential for maintaining physical and mental well-being. By prioritizing self-care you enhance productivity reduce stress and improve overall satisfaction with your work and personal life.

6. Learn to say no: It's common to feel obligated to say yes to every request or demand placed upon you but this can lead to overcommitment and feeling overwhelmed. Learn to say no when a request doesn't align with your priorities or when you feel it would compromise your boundaries or well-being. Saying no respectfully and assertively allows you to maintain focus on your priorities and avoid spreading yourself too thin.

7. Schedule and manage your time effectively: Create a schedule or use a planner to allocate time for specific tasks and activities. Prioritize your most important and challenging tasks during your most productive periods when you're likely to have higher energy levels and concentration. Break your day into blocks of focused work time interspersed with short breaks to rest and recharge.

8. Review and adapt: Regularly review your task list priorities and time-management strategies. Assess what's working and what needs improvement. Be flexible and willing to adapt your

approach to changing circumstances. By regularly evaluating and adjusting your strategies you can optimize your productivity and maintain an effective workflow.

Examples:

1. Establishing Healthy Boundaries with Others:

Example 1: In a working environment a colleague consistently interrupts you while you're trying to concentrate. You can establish a boundary by politely stating "I appreciate your input but I need uninterrupted time to focus on my tasks. Could we discuss this at a more suitable time perhaps during our scheduled meeting?"

Example 2: You have a relative who constantly asks for financial assistance impacting your own financial stability. To establish a boundary you can kindly say "I care about your well-being but I need to prioritize my own financial goals at the moment. I won't be able to provide further assistance but I can help you explore other options."

2. Prioritizing Tasks and Managing Time Effectively:

Example 1: You have a project deadline approaching but you're also responsible for household chores. By prioritizing and managing your time effectively you can allocate specific hours in your schedule to focus solely on the project. You can delegate some of the household tasks to other family members or ask for their help.

Example 2: You're overwhelmed with your workload and personal commitments. By practicing effective time management you identify tasks that can be delegated or postponed. You communicate your priorities to your team or colleagues seeking their support in redistributing tasks. By setting boundaries on your time and learning to say no you regain control and focus on your high-priority tasks.

In conclusion setting healthy boundaries with others and prioritizing tasks and managing time effectively are critical skills for personal and professional success. Establishing clear boundaries allows you to protect your well-being and maintain healthy relationships while effective time management ensures that you achieve your goals and maximize productivity. By implementing the strategies and examples provided in this chapter you can create a balanced and fulfilling life.

Chapter 7: Embracing Imperfection

Introduction:

In a world that often values perfection it can be challenging to let go of our perfectionistic tendencies and embrace imperfection. However this chapter will explore the benefits of letting go of perfectionism and how embracing mistakes can lead to growth and learning. By understanding the detrimental effects of perfectionism and reframing our perspective on mistakes we can cultivate a healthier and more productive mindset.

Letting Go of Perfectionism:

Perfectionism is the pursuit of flawlessness and the refusal to accept anything less. It can manifest in various aspects of our lives be it in work relationships or personal goals. While striving for excellence can be a positive motivator perfectionism becomes problematic when it leads to unrealistic expectations self-criticism and an inability to appreciate progress.

One of the first steps in letting go of perfectionism is recognizing its negative impact on our well-being. Perfectionism often creates a constant state of stress and anxiety as we strive to meet impossible standards. This chronic stress can take a toll on our mental and physical health leading to burnout low self-esteem and even depression.

To break free from perfectionism we must challenge our beliefs and redefine what success means to us. Instead of striving for an unattainable ideal we can set realistic and meaningful goals that align with our values and passions. Embracing imperfection allows us to embrace our authentic selves and find joy in the journey rather than solely focusing on the destination.

Embracing Mistakes and Learning from Them:
   Mistakes are an inevitable part of life but they are also opportunities for growth and learning. By embracing mistakes we can shift our perspective from seeing them as failures to viewing them as valuable stepping stones on our path to success.

When we make a mistake it is important to remember that we are human and that no one is perfect. Rather than beating ourselves up over our shortcomings we should approach them with self-compassion and understanding. It is through mistakes that we gain valuable insights acquire new skills and develop resilience.

Learning from mistakes involves reflecting on what went wrong and identifying areas for improvement. This process of self-reflection allows us to gain a deeper understanding of ourselves and our abilities ultimately leading to personal growth. By embracing mistakes we can also develop a growth mindset which emphasizes the belief that our abilities can be developed through dedication and hard work.

To illustrate the concept of embracing mistakes and learning from them let's consider an example:

Sarah a graphic designer has been working on a project for a client. She has spent several hours perfecting the design ensuring every line and color is flawless. However when she presents her work to the client they express disappointment feeling that something is missing.

Initially Sarah feels devastated and experiences a sense of failure. However she takes a moment to reflect and realizes that this mistake can be an opportunity for growth. She acknowledges that her perfectionistic tendencies led her to overlook the client's specific requirements and focused too much on the aesthetics.

Sarah decides to learn from this mistake by reaching out to the client for feedback. She actively listens to their concerns and asks for clarification on their expectations. Through this process Sarah gains a better understanding of the client's vision and realizes that she needs to strike a balance between aesthetics and meeting the client's needs.

With this newfound knowledge Sarah revisits the project and makes the necessary adjustments. She communicates openly with the client ensuring that she addresses their concerns and incorporates their vision into the design. Through this experience Sarah not only improves her skills as a graphic designer but also strengthens her client relationships.

In this example Sarah demonstrates the power of embracing mistakes and turning them into opportunities for growth. Instead of dwelling on her initial failure she uses it as a chance to learn improve and develop a stronger professional approach.

Conclusion:

Embracing imperfection and learning from mistakes are essential components of personal and professional growth. By letting go of perfectionism we can alleviate the stress and anxiety associated with unrealistic expectations. Instead we can focus on setting meaningful goals and appreciating the progress we make along the way.

Mistakes though often seen as failures are invaluable opportunities for learning and self-improvement. By reframing our perspective on mistakes we can cultivate a growth mindset and approach challenges with resilience and self-compassion. Through self-reflection and a willingness to embrace imperfections we can harness the power of mistakes to propel us towards our goals.

Remember it's okay to make mistakes. They are not a reflection of our worth but rather stepping stones on our journey to success. Embracing imperfection allows us to live a more fulfilling and empowered life.

Chapter 8: Engaging in Relaxation and Stress-Reduction Techniques

Introduction:

In today's fast-paced and demanding world stress has become an unavoidable part of our lives. The constant pressure from work relationships and other responsibilities can lead to excessive worry and overthinking. These negative thought patterns can be detrimental to our mental well-being and overall quality of life. However by incorporating relaxation and stress-reduction techniques into our daily routine we can effectively manage stress and prevent overthinking. This chapter will delve deep into various activities and practices that can promote relaxation and reduce stress levels.

Section 1: Importance of Managing Stress

1.1 The Impact of Stress on Mental Health:

Stress when left unmanaged can have severe consequences on our mental health. Continuous exposure to stressors can lead to anxiety disorders depression poor decision-making and decreased cognitive functioning. Managing stress is crucial to ensure optimal mental well-being and prevent the development of mental health issues.

1.2 The Role of Overthinking:

Overthinking is a common response to stress. It involves repetitively dwelling on negative thoughts and scenarios which can exacerbate stress levels and hinder problem-solving abilities. Overthinking often leads to a vicious cycle where stress triggers overthinking and overthinking intensifies stress. Managing stress effectively can break this cycle and reduce the tendency for overthinking.

Section 2: Relaxation Techniques for Stress Reduction

2.1 Deep Breathing Exercises:

Deep breathing exercises are simple yet effective techniques to induce relaxation and reduce stress. By taking slow deep breaths we activate the body's natural relaxation response leading to a decrease in heart rate and blood pressure. One such exercise is diaphragmatic breathing where you inhale deeply through your nose allowing your abdomen to rise and exhale slowly through your mouth allowing your abdomen to fall. Practicing deep breathing exercises for several minutes each day can significantly reduce stress levels.

2.2 Progressive Muscle Relaxation (PMR):

Progressive muscle relaxation is a technique that involves tensing and then relaxing different muscle groups systematically. By consciously tensing and releasing specific muscle groups PMR helps achieve a state of deep relaxation and counters the physical manifestations of stress. Starting from the toes and working up to the head one can progressively relax each muscle group. Regular PMR practice can result in decreased muscle tension and overall stress reduction.

2.3 Meditation:

Meditation is a powerful practice that promotes relaxation mindfulness and emotional well-being. Various forms of meditation such as mindfulness meditation transcendental meditation and loving-kindness meditation are available. Mindfulness meditation involves focusing on the present moment observing thoughts and sensations without judgment. Regular meditation practice has been found to reduce stress improve attention span and enhance overall mental well-being.

2.4 Mindfulness-Based Stress Reduction (MBSR):

Developed by Jon Kabat-Zinn MBSR combines mindfulness meditation and yoga to foster stress reduction. By incorporating mindfulness into daily activities MBSR helps individuals become more aware of their thoughts emotions and physical sensations. This heightened awareness enables individuals to respond to stressors in a more mindful and effective manner. MBSR programs often include guided meditation gentle yoga and discussions on stress management techniques.

2.5 Guided Imagery:

Guided imagery is a relaxation technique that involves creating vivid mental images to evoke a sense of calm and relaxation. By visualizing peaceful or desired scenarios individuals can redirect their attention from stressors and induce a state of relaxation. Guided imagery can be self-guided through recorded audio or facilitated by a professional. It has been found effective in reducing stress anxiety and pain.

Section 3: Stress-Reducing Activities and Practices

3.1 Physical Exercise:

Regular physical exercise has numerous benefits for stress reduction. Engaging in activities like jogging swimming yoga or dancing helps release endorphins the brain's "feel-good" chemicals. These endorphins act as natural stress and pain relievers. Exercise also promotes better sleep increased self-confidence and improved mood all of which contribute to stress reduction.

3.2 Engaging Hobbies:

Participating in hobbies and activities that bring joy and fulfillment can be an excellent way to reduce stress. Creative pursuits like painting writing playing musical instruments gardening or cooking can serve as outlets for self-expression and relaxation. These activities divert attention from stressors provide a sense of accomplishment and enhance overall well-being.

3.3 Social Support:

Building and maintaining strong social connections can significantly reduce stress levels. Engaging in meaningful relationships whether with friends family or support groups provides emotional support a sense of belonging and opportunities for open communication. Sharing concerns and seeking advice from trusted individuals can alleviate stress and promote emotional well-being.

3.4 Time Management:

Effective time management is essential for stress reduction.

By prioritizing tasks setting realistic goals and creating a structured schedule individuals can avoid feeling overwhelmed and reduce stress levels. Breaking down large tasks into smaller manageable ones and practicing efficient time allocation can lead to increased productivity and decreased stress.

3.5 Self-Care:

Engaging in self-care activities is vital for stress reduction. Taking time to care for oneself physically emotionally and mentally can recharge energy reserves and promote relaxation. Self-care practices can include getting enough sleep eating a balanced diet practicing mindfulness journaling taking relaxing baths or indulging in leisure activities.

Conclusion:

Incorporating relaxation and stress-reduction techniques into our lives plays a vital role in managing stress levels and preventing overthinking. By practicing deep breathing exercises progressive muscle relaxation meditation mindfulness-based stress reduction and guided imagery individuals can induce relaxation responses and reduce the physiological and psychological effects of stress. Engaging in stress-reducing activities like physical exercise hobbies social support time management and self-care promotes overall well-being and contributes to a healthier more balanced life. Start integrating these techniques and activities into your routine and watch as your stress levels decrease providing you with a greater sense of peace and tranquility.

Chapter 9: Seeking Support and Connection

Building a Supportive Network

In our journey through life one of the most valuable resources we can have is a supportive network of people who can uplift and empower us. Building and maintaining this network requires effort but the rewards are immeasurable. In this chapter we will explore strategies for building a supportive network and understanding the importance of seeking connection with others.

1. Identify Your Support Needs

Before you can build a supportive network it's important to understand your own support needs. Take some time to reflect on the areas of your life where you could benefit from support. These could include emotional support professional advice guidance or practical assistance. By identifying your needs you can proactively seek out individuals who can provide the support you require.

For example if you are starting a new business venture you might seek out mentors or industry professionals who can offer guidance and expertise. Alternatively if you're going through a challenging time emotionally you might want to connect with friends or family members who can provide a listening ear and offer emotional support.

2. Leverage Existing Relationships

Building a supportive network doesn't mean starting from scratch. Often the foundation for a supportive network begins with the relationships you already have. Friends family members colleagues and acquaintances can all be valuable sources of support if you communicate your needs effectively.

Start by evaluating your existing relationships and consider who you feel comfortable confiding in and seeking support from. Then make an effort to nurture these relationships by spending time together engaging in meaningful conversations and offering support in return. By strengthening the bonds with those who are already in your life you can further develop your supportive network.

3. Seek Out Like-minded Individuals

In addition to leveraging existing relationships it's important to actively seek out like-minded individuals who share similar interests goals or values. These connections can bring a deeper level of understanding and support for your journey.

Consider joining clubs organizations or online communities

related to your interests or aspirations. In these groups you can find people who are on a similar path and who can offer valuable insights encouragement and support. By surrounding yourself with individuals who share your passions or ambitions you create an environment that fosters growth and mutual support.

For example if you are interested in photography joining a photography club can provide you with a supportive network of fellow photographers who can offer feedback on your work and share their own experiences and knowledge. This shared interest can foster a strong bond and provide a valuable support system.

4. Embrace Vulnerability

Building a supportive network requires vulnerability. It involves openly sharing your experiences struggles and aspirations with others. This vulnerability allows others to connect with you on a deeper level and offer the support you need.

While vulnerability can be challenging it is essential for cultivating meaningful connections. Start by gradually opening up to individuals you trust. Share your thoughts and emotions and allow yourself to be authentic and genuine. In turn others will be more likely to reciprocate and offer their support and understanding.

5. Consistency and Reciprocity

Building a supportive network is an ongoing process that requires consistency and reciprocity. Make an effort to consistently reach out to individuals in your network showing genuine interest in their lives and offering support when needed. By being a supportive friend or colleague you can cultivate strong relationships that will be there for you when you need them.

Remember that support is a two-way street. Be open to receiving support from others but also be willing to offer your support to them when they need it. This reciprocity strengthens the bonds within your network and creates a culture of mutual support.

Communicating Your Needs with Loved Ones

Once you have built a supportive network it's important to effectively communicate your needs with your loved ones. Clear and open communication is key to receiving the support you require and maintaining healthy relationships. Here are some strategies for communicating your needs effectively:

1. Self-Awareness and Reflection

Before communicating your needs take some time for self-reflection. Gain clarity on what you truly need and how you can express it to others. It's important to be specific about your needs and to understand how they can be met. This self-awareness allows you to communicate your needs more effectively and reduces the chances of misunderstanding or unmet expectations.

2. Choose the Right Time and Place

When seeking support from your loved ones it's important

to choose an appropriate time and place for the conversation. Ensure that you have their undivided attention and that you are in a comfortable and private setting. This creates a safe space for open and honest communication.

For example instead of discussing a sensitive matter in a crowded restaurant opt for a quiet and relaxed setting where both parties can focus on the conversation without distractions.

3. Use "I" Statements

When communicating your needs using "I" statements can be more effective than blaming or accusatory language. "I" statements express your own feelings needs and desires without placing blame on the other person. This approach promotes understanding and empathy and reduces defensiveness.

For example instead of saying "You never listen to me you could say "I feel unheard when I share my thoughts and would appreciate it if you could give me your full attention."

4. Be Clear and Direct

To avoid misunderstandings it's crucial to be clear and direct when communicating your needs. Clearly express what you need and how the other person can support you. Avoid vague or ambiguous statements that may lead to confusion.

For instance if you need emotional support you could say "I've been feeling down lately and I could really use someone to talk to. Would you be available to listen to me for a while?"

5. Express Gratitude and Appreciation

When someone provides support and meets your needs it's important to express gratitude and appreciation. This acknowledgment not only strengthens the bond between you and your loved ones but also encourages them to continue supporting you.

Take the time to thank your loved ones for their support whether it's through words gestures or acts of kindness. Let them know how much their support means to you and how it has positively impacted your life.

Conclusion

Building a supportive network and effectively communicating your needs are essential skills for seeking support and connection. By identifying your support needs leveraging existing relationships seeking out like-minded individuals embracing vulnerability and practicing consistency and reciprocity you can build a strong network of support. Additionally by practicing self-awareness choosing the right time and place using "I" statements being clear and direct and expressing gratitude and appreciation you can effectively communicate your needs with your loved ones. Through these strategies you can foster meaningful connections and receive the support you need for a fulfilling and empowered life.

Chapter 10: Cultivating Gratitude and Positive Thinking

In this chapter we will delve into the concepts of cultivating gratitude and positive thinking. These two practices have been found to have numerous benefits for our mental and emotional well-being. By incorporating gratitude and positive thinking into our daily lives we can experience increased happiness improved relationships and enhanced overall life satisfaction.

Section 1: Fostering Gratefulness in Everyday Life

Gratitude is the practice of acknowledging and appreciating the good things in our lives. It involves recognizing the positive aspects of our experiences relationships and the world around us. The act of expressing gratitude can be done through various methods such as journaling speaking aloud or simply reflecting silently.

1.1 Gratitude Journaling

One effective way to foster gratefulness is through gratitude journaling. This practice involves regularly writing down the things we are grateful for. By putting our gratitude into written words we enhance our ability to fully appreciate and remember the positive aspects of our lives. A gratitude journal can be as simple as a notebook or a dedicated app on your phone. Set aside a few minutes each day to write down three to five things you are grateful for. These can range from small everyday occurrences such as a delicious meal or a sunny day to meaningful relationships and personal achievements.

For example imagine you had a difficult day at work but you managed to have a pleasant conversation with a coworker during your lunch break. By journaling about this positive interaction you shift your focus from the challenges of your day to the joy of connecting with others.

1.2 Expressing Gratitude to Others

Another way to cultivate gratitude is by expressing it to others. Take the time to thank people for their kindness support or any positive impact they have had on your life. This can be done through a simple thank-you note a verbal expression of appreciation or even a small gesture of kindness in return.

For instance suppose a friend takes the time to lend you a helping hand when you're moving to a new home. By expressing your gratitude and offering to help them with something in return you not only show your appreciation but also strengthen your bond and foster a sense of reciprocal gratitude.

1.3 Shifting Perspective through Gratitude

Practicing gratitude can also help shift our perspective from focusing on what's lacking in our lives to appreciating what we already have. When we are able to see the positive aspects of our experiences we become more resilient and optimistic.

For example imagine you are going through a challenging time in your career and you feel stuck and unmotivated. By reflecting on the skills and opportunities you have been given you can shift your perspective and find gratitude for the growth and learning that has come from these experiences. This shift in mindset can lead to increased motivation and a renewed sense of purpose.

Section 2: Harnessing the Power of Positive Thinking

Positive thinking is a mindset that focuses on finding the good in every situation. It involves consciously choosing to interpret events and circumstances in a positive light rather than dwelling on the negatives. By adopting a positive thinking approach we can enhance our overall well-being and improve our capacity to handle challenges.

2.1 Reframing Negative Thoughts

One way to harness the power of positive thinking is by reframing negative thoughts. When we encounter a negative event or experience we can choose to reinterpret it in a way that focuses on the positive aspects or the potential for growth.

For instance suppose you receive feedback at work that highlights areas for improvement. Instead of viewing it as criticism you can reframe it as an opportunity for personal and professional development. By reframing the feedback in a positive light you can maintain a positive outlook and approach the situation with a growth mindset.

2.2 Cultivating Positive Self-Talk

Positive self-talk is the practice of using uplifting and encouraging language when speaking to ourselves. It involves replacing negative and self-limiting thoughts with positive affirmations and supportive statements. By cultivating positive self-talk we can boost our self-confidence increase our resilience and improve our overall mental well-being.

For example imagine you made a mistake on a project at work and you start to berate yourself for the error. Instead of dwelling on self-criticism practice positive self-talk by reminding yourself of your past successes and believing in your ability to learn from mistakes. This shift in self-perception can help you approach future challenges with optimism and self-assuredness.

2.3 Surrounding Yourself with Positivity

Another aspect of harnessing the power of positive thinking is by surrounding ourselves with positivity. This can involve seeking out supportive and positive people engaging in activities that bring us joy and creating an environment that fosters optimism and gratitude.

For instance suppose you find that spending time with certain individuals consistently drains your energy and affects your mood negatively. By consciously choosing to surround yourself with positive and uplifting people you can create a supportive network that encourages positive thinking and reinforces your own growth and happiness.

Conclusion

Cultivating gratitude and positive thinking is a powerful way to enhance our overall well-being and lead happier lives. By fostering gratefulness we shift our perspective from focusing on what's lacking to appreciating what we have. Harnessing the power of positive thinking allows us to reframe negative thoughts cultivate positive self-talk and surround ourselves with positivity. By incorporating these practices into our daily routines we can cultivate a mindset that is more resilient optimistic and appreciative of the good in our lives.

Tips for Stop Worrying

1. Identify the source: Take some time to think about what is causing you to worry. Is it work-related a personal relationship or something else entirely? Understanding the source can help you address the specific issue.

2. Accept uncertainty: Recognize that some things are beyond your control and that uncertainty is a natural part of life. Trying to control every outcome will only lead to more worry.

3. Practice mindfulness: Engage in activities that bring you back to the present moment such as meditation or deep breathing exercises. This can help you focus on what is happening now rather than worrying about the future.

4. Challenge your thoughts: When you catch yourself in a cycle of worrying thoughts ask yourself if there is evidence to support them. Often our worries are based on irrational fears or worst-case scenarios.

5. Take small steps: Break down the problem or situation into smaller manageable tasks. By tackling them one at a time you can lessen the feeling of overwhelm and gradually make progress.

6. Prioritize self-care: Take care of your physical and emotional well-being. Get enough sleep eat a balanced diet exercise regularly and engage in activities that bring you joy and relaxation.

7. Limit your exposure to news and social media: Constant exposure to negative news and social media can amplify worries. Set boundaries and give yourself breaks from these platforms to reduce anxiety.

8. Seek support: Reach out to trusted friends family members or a therapist to talk about your worries. Sometimes just sharing your concerns with someone can alleviate the anxiety.

9. Focus on problem-solving: Instead of just worrying take proactive steps to address the issue at hand. Try brainstorming solutions and create an action plan to work towards a resolution.

10. Practice self-compassion: Be kind to yourself and remind yourself that it's okay to feel worried sometimes. Treat yourself with the same compassion you would extend to a friend in need.

11. Get organized: Create a to-do list or a schedule to keep track of your tasks and commitments. Having a clear plan can help reduce worry about forgetting something important.

12. Engage in relaxation techniques: Explore various relaxation techniques like yoga progressive muscle relaxation or guided imagery to calm your mind and relax your body.

13. Challenge catastrophic thinking: Avoid jumping to the worst-case scenario. Instead focus on potential positive outcomes or

more realistic alternatives.

14. Limit caffeine intake: Excess caffeine can exacerbate feelings of anxiety and make you more prone to worry. Consider cutting back or switching to decaffeinated options.

15. Take breaks and recharge: Give yourself regular breaks throughout the day to engage in activities that help you relax and recharge. This can help prevent burnout and reduce worry.

16. Practice gratitude: Take time each day to write down things you are grateful for. Shifting your focus to the positive aspects of your life can help counteract worry.

17. Engage in hobbies: Find activities or hobbies that bring you joy and provide a healthy distraction from worrying thoughts. Immersing yourself in something you enjoy can reduce anxiety.

18. Set realistic expectations: Be honest with yourself about what is realistically achievable. Setting unrealistic expectations can lead to unnecessary worry and disappointment.

19. Develop a support network: Surround yourself with positive and supportive people who can offer guidance and reassurance when you need it.

20. Establish healthy boundaries: Learn to say no when necessary and set boundaries to protect your time and energy. Overcommitting can lead to increased worry and stress.

21. Practice positive self-talk: Replace negative and self-critical

thoughts with positive affirmations. Remind yourself of your strengths and accomplishments to boost your confidence.

22. Learn stress management techniques: Explore different stress management techniques such as deep breathing exercises mindfulness or journaling to help reduce overall stress levels.

23. Get regular exercise: Physical activity releases endorphins which are natural mood boosters. Regular exercise can help alleviate anxiety and worry.

24. Practice time management: Prioritize tasks set realistic deadlines and break down large projects into smaller manageable steps. Effective time management can help reduce worry about getting things done.

25. Keep a worry journal: Write down your worries and fears in a journal. This can help you gain perspective identify recurring patterns and find potential solutions.

26. Challenge perfectionism: Striving for perfection can fuel worry and anxiety. Recognize that nobody is perfect and it's okay to make mistakes or have imperfections.

27. Take care of your physical health: Engaging in regular medical check-ups and maintaining a healthy lifestyle can help reduce worry about physical ailments.

28. Seek professional help if needed: If your worries become overwhelming and start interfering with your daily life consider seeking help from a mental health professional.

29. Practice deep breathing: Deep breathing exercises activate the relaxation response and can help calm an anxious mind. Take slow deep breaths filling your lungs completely and exhale slowly.

30. Create a worry-free zone: Designate a specific time and place to express your worries. Outside of that designated time make a conscious effort to redirect your thoughts to more positive and productive topics.

31. Focus on the present moment: Instead of getting caught up in hypothetical future scenarios focus on what you can do right now. Take small steps towards your goals and trust the process.

32. Challenge the need for control: Recognize that you cannot control everything and that it's okay to let go of things that are beyond your control. Focus on what you can influence instead.

33. Practice self-compassion: Treat yourself with kindness and understanding. Remember that everyone makes mistakes and experiences setbacks. Remind yourself that worrying does not solve problems but self-care can.

34. Develop a relaxation routine: Create a routine that incorporates relaxation techniques such as meditation yoga or taking relaxing baths. Regularly engaging in these practices can help reduce overall levels of worry.

35. Reframe negative thoughts: Recognize negative or worrying thoughts and challenge them. Look for evidence to support a more positive or realistic perspective.

36. Engage in positive self-reflection: Take some time to reflect on your past successes and personal growth. Remind yourself of all the challenges you have overcome which can provide reassurance for future situations.

37. Practice time-limited worrying: Set aside a specific amount of time each day to actively worry and ruminate. When that time is up consciously redirect your thoughts to more positive or productive activities.

38. Avoid excessive reassurance-seeking: Constantly seeking reassurance from others can create a cycle of dependency and reinforce worry. Learn to trust your own judgment and seek reassurance from within.

39. Challenge the need for certainty: Worry often stems from a desire for certainty in an uncertain world. Embrace the inherent uncertainty of life and trust in your ability to navigate challenges as they arise.

40. Engage in regular exercise: Physical activity releases endorphins which can help boost your mood and reduce anxiety. Find an exercise routine that you enjoy and make it a regular part of your schedule.

41. Take breaks from technology: Constant exposure to screens and notifications can contribute to feelings of overwhelm and worry. Set aside designated screen-free time to disconnect and recharge.

42. Identify triggers: Pay attention to situations people or

environments that tend to trigger your worries. Once you identify these triggers you can develop strategies to reduce their impact or avoid them when possible.

43. Practice realistic optimism: Cultivate a positive outlook while maintaining a realistic perspective. Focus on potential solutions and opportunities rather than dwelling on potential problems.

44. Break the worry cycle: When you catch yourself getting caught in a cycle of worry try interrupting the pattern by engaging in a different activity or distraction. This can help break the cycle and redirect your thoughts.

45. Engage in grounding exercises: Grounding exercises help bring your attention back to the present moment and your immediate surroundings. Use your senses to focus on what you can see hear touch taste and smell.

46. Challenge the urge to overanalyze: Resist the temptation to overanalyze every situation. Recognize when you have gathered enough information and trust in your ability to make decisions.

47. Set realistic goals: Break down larger goals into smaller achievable milestones. Setting realistic goals can help you stay focused and reduce worry about accomplishing a massive undertaking.

48. Practice acceptance: Learn to accept what you cannot change. Understand that certain situations or outcomes may be beyond your control and it's more productive to focus on

adapting and finding solutions.

49. Surround yourself with positive influences: Spend time with supportive and positive people who encourage and uplift you. Avoid spending excessive time with individuals who consistently fuel your worries.

50. Create a worry box: Write down your worries on slips of paper and place them in a designated box. This can help symbolize mentally letting go of your worries and giving yourself permission to set them aside temporarily.

51. Get enough sleep: Lack of sleep can increase feelings of stress and worry. Develop a consistent sleep routine and prioritize getting enough rest to support your overall well-being.

52. Practice self-reflection: Spend time reflecting on your worries and the root causes behind them. Understanding the underlying reasons can help you address them more effectively.

53. Engage in daily affirmations: Repeat positive affirmations to yourself regularly. Focus on statements that empower and encourage you reminding yourself of your strengths and resilience.

54. Engage in creative outlets: Explore creative activities like painting writing or playing music to express and process your worries. Creative outlets can provide a healthy release and help shift your focus.

55. Challenge the need for constant productivity: Recognize that downtime and relaxation are also essential components of

a balanced life. Allow yourself time to rest and recharge without guilt.

56. Seek perspective from others: Discuss your worries with trusted individuals who can provide an outside perspective. Sometimes others may offer insights or alternative viewpoints that can alleviate your worries.

57. Practice acceptance of uncertainty: Acknowledge that not everything can be predicted or controlled. Embracing uncertainty can help you let go of the need for complete certainty and reduce worry.

58. Engage in positive distractions: Find activities that can take your mind off worries and bring you joy or relaxation. This could be reading a book going for a walk or engaging in a hobby you enjoy.

59. Identify your support system: Recognize the people in your life who can offer support and a listening ear when you need it. Build and nurture these relationships to have a strong support system in place.

60. Develop a gratitude practice: Regularly express gratitude for the positive aspects of your life. This can shift your focus from worry to appreciation enhancing overall well-being.

61. Learn relaxation techniques: Explore various relaxation techniques such as deep breathing progressive muscle relaxation or guided imagery to help calm your mind and alleviate worry.

62. Challenge cognitive distortions: Recognize and challenge common thinking patterns such as overgeneralization catastrophizing or filtering out positive experiences. Replace them with more balanced and realistic thinking.

63. Practice self-soothing techniques: Identify techniques that help you calm down when feeling anxious or worried. This could include listening to calming music taking a warm bath or engaging in soothing activities like coloring or knitting.

64. Develop a positive morning routine: Start your day with positive habits that set the tone for a calm and productive day. This could include meditation journaling or engaging in a physical activity you enjoy.

65. Practice assertiveness: Learn to assert yourself and express your needs and boundaries in a respectful manner. Being assertive can help reduce worry about being taken advantage of or not being able to advocate for yourself.

66. Learn from your worries: Reflect on the lessons you can learn from your worries. Sometimes worries can reveal areas where you need to grow make changes or set healthier boundaries.